The Prairie Girl Stories

Our
Swedish Heritage

Janet Moen

Copyright © 2021 Janet Moen
All rights reserved.

ISBN: 978-1-62269-037-4

Who Will Tell Your Stories To The Next Generation?

Write Heart Memories®

Ultimate Workbooks, Published Stories & Interviews With Beth Lord
Preserving Legacy & You In A Book

206-929-0024 | www.bethlord.com | beth@bethlord.com

THE PRAIRIE GIRL STORIES

The true stories of a young girl's prairie life in Canada during the early 1900's.

Out on the prairie that's all there was…that's all I knew.

~ Irene

Janet Moen

For my mother Irene, 1910-2007.

Janet Moen

CONTENTS

1. Introduction 11
2. Homesteaders 13
3. Little House on the Canadian Prairie 19
4. The Oxen 23
5. Quicksand 25
6. Prairie Chips 27
7. Queenie and Tootsie 29
8. Storms 31
9. Rhymes and Riddles from Hilda's Trunk 33
10. Prairie Mushrooms and Wildflowers 39
11. Wild Strawberries 41
12. Chokecherries and Saskatoons 43
13. Up to No Good 45
14. The Goosebone (Poem) From Hilda's Trunk ... 47
15. The Blizzard 49
16. Winter 51
17. Apple Peelings 57
18. Wolves 59
19. A Country Girl (Poem) From Hilda's Trunk 61
20. The Basket Social Barn Dances 63
21. The One-Room Prairie School 65
22. Freehand Paper Cutting Contest 69
23. Gypsies 71
24. Gopher Tails 73
25. World War I Flu 75
26. Goodbye Prairie 77
27. The Sod House and Barn Owl 79
28. The Long Journey to Seattle 81
29. The Rock Children 85
30. Photos from The Prairie Girl Stories 87

Acknowledgements

A great big "Thank You" to my family, friends, and relatives for your enthusiasm, interest, patience, and help for this little book - I want to thank all of you from the bottom of my heart!

1   INTRODUCTION

The Prairie Girl Stories is about my mother's life when she was a little girl who lived with her family on the unsettled Canadian prairie. Her name was Irene.

Over one hundred years ago, Elna Irene Rosenberg was born in Seattle, Washington, and moved to the Saskatchewan prairie when she was only one year old, and her brother Roy was just an infant. Her brother Adolf joined their family on the prairie when Irene was four years old, and her sister, Violet, was born in Seattle after they left the prairie when Irene was nine years old.

Growing up I loved to hear the stories that Grandma and my mom would tell. When I was a little girl the prairie stories were as much loved as my nursery rhymes and fairy tale books. In my mother's late years, she and I spent many enjoyable hours reliving those early years of her life. Her memories were still as vivid as if they had just happened. My mother and her family truly lived the pioneer life from 1911-1919 while homesteading on the vast Saskatchewan prairie in Canada. These are her stories…

But the stories first have to begin earlier in the late 1800s when my grandmother Hilda, Irene's mother was a little girl just arriving from Sweden…

The following stories and Swedish family history are a gift from Hilda, Irene and myself to you. Mom expressed that she would be deeply honored if I'd compile her stories into a little book to be passed down and remembered. Lovingly, I've chosen The Prairie Girl Stories as its title.

Janet Siepmann Moen
Kirkland, Washington
August 2021

2 HOMESTEADERS

Discovered among my grandmother's papers and penciled in one of her journals, Hilda had written the following:

"Hilda Jacobson was born in Sweden, February 19, 1889. Came to America at the age of two years. Mother died nine months after we came over here. Father left us three children, my sister 6 years old my brother 4 years old. We were then given away to whoever would take us. Mr. & Mrs. Anders Olson took me and raised me until I was 15. Then I went out to work, worked out until February 27, 1910. I then married Oscar G. Rosenberg."

Hilda and Oscar

The Red River Valley of the Dakotas is known as the "Wheat Belt of North America." Before the turn of the century, Nils Jacobsson, Hilda's father, emigrated from Fränninge, Sweden, a small village in southern Sweden, and settled in the Red River Valley area of North Dakota to farm in a new land. Shortly after, his wife Elna, three children, Ada, Olaf and Hilda, and Nils' brother Peter, followed. But after tragically losing his wife from pneumonia and having to 'farm out' his children, Nils migrated to the Saskatchewan prairie where he filed a homestead claim, built a sod house and worked the land – mostly raising wheat. He traveled back and forth to Dakota to visit his children when he could.

Anders and Elna Olson, who took little Hilda in had emigrated from southern Sweden ten years earlier with four children and settled on a homestead claim in the Red River Valley, in what was still Dakota Territory. On this large 560-acre wheat farm near Harwood and Argusville, on the outskirts of Fargo, is where Hilda grew up. The Olsons were a hard-working Swedish family with very old-country ways. Hilda remembers wearing wooden shoes when she was very young. She also remembers her big sister, Ada, living on an adjoining farm, and faithfully walking every evening to visit her. Then she stopped coming. She learned later that Ada, like their mother, had died of pneumonia. Ada was ten years old. Hilda was too young to remember her mother, Elna Jacobsson, and longed to see a picture of her, but there were none.

Hilda loved school. All the days of her life she saved her meticulously hand-written lesson books, each one a labor of love and a work of art. The small one-room Rush River Schoolhouse was about a quarter mile east of the Olson farm. When Hilda started school in the first grade, she could only speak Swedish. In this little country school, she learned to speak English and she learned to read and write in Swedish and English, as the pupils were schooled in both languages. In 1897 when Hilda was eight years old, a School Souvenir presented by her teacher, Miss Ella O'Brien, lists Hilda Jacobson and the names of thirteen schoolmates.

At lunchtime Hilda would have to hurry home, rig-up the horse and wagon and drive lunch out to the farm workers, then unhitch and hurry back to school before the teacher rang the school bell. For Hilda to get the leather harness straps up on the horse's back, she would have to stand on a wooden box because she wasn't tall enough to reach.

The Olson's sons, John and Andrew, worked mostly in the wheat fields and daughters, Hannah and Christina, helped with the chores inside the big farmhouse. Little Hilda was, as she called herself, "the barnyard girl." She would have liked to help with the inside chores but as soon as she was able, it was her duty to help milk the cows, water and care for the farm animals and work outside in the garden.

John Olson was her favorite. He took a special interest in her and when he went to town he often would bring her back a little gift of a new pencil or an apple. She really liked the pencil and dreamed of someday becoming a secretary.

Hilda's brother, Olaf, grew up about five miles away on a farm in the nearby Prosper area. When Olaf became a young man, he changed his last name from Jacobson to Nelson. By adding 'son' to his father's first name, Olaf's last name became Nel-son, which is an old Swedish custom. (Nils Jacobsson and Nilsson is the Swedish spelling.) At about the time Hilda left home at age fifteen to go to work, she didn't think it seemed right for her brother to have a different last name, so she changed her name to Nelson, too. In those days there were few official records kept.

Hilda's first job away from home was working for a widower who had a little girl and a nice farm. Hilda liked the little girl named Ida and the buggy horse, Prince, and the farm, but the widower not so much. So, in the night, she quietly packed her things and pedaled her bicycle all of the twenty-five miles to Fargo where she got a job working and cooking at the large boarding house and restaurant called *The Travelers Home*. It was located at 124 First Avenue South in Fargo, North Dakota. Many Swedish immigrants stopped there.

For the next five years this is where Hilda lived and worked, and this is where she met her future husband, Oscar George Rosenberg. (Oskar Georg is the Swedish spelling.) He was a Swedish immigrant bound for Harwood, North Dakota, (a Swedish community) who arrived at *Ellis Island* with two friends, a butcher and a laborer, on the British ocean liner RMS *Carmania* in the spring of 1907. From New York's terminal, with still more than a thousand miles to go, they traveled by train to North Dakota. Oscar said the worst part of the whole journey coming from Sweden was crossing the North Sea, saying they had experienced a terrible storm with very high winds and giant waves! He said having crossed three bodies of water and had traveled miles and miles of railway, North Dakota was a long, long way from Sweden! His family was from the very small village of Löderup in Skåne County by the Baltic Sea in southern Sweden. The ship's manifest lists "joiner" as his occupation. ('Snickarimästar' in Swedish – 'Master Carpenter' in English.)

Oscar's first work in America was at a large lumber camp by Deer River and Spring Lake in northern Minnesota, almost two hundred miles from Fargo. He wasn't happy with the job and heard talk of carpentry work in Seattle, Washington.

After courting and asking Hilda for her hand in marriage, Oscar wanted to head out West to Seattle, to check the city and the carpentry work. In 1909, Seattle was preparing for the *Alaska-Yukon-Pacific Exposition,* acclaimed "The Most Beautiful Exposition Ever Held," and was alive with activity. Oscar wrote Hilda from Seattle and told of all these things. So joyfully, the bride to be, packed up her trunk, said goodbye to her brother Olaf, to the Olsons, and to her lifelong friends in North Dakota. Hilda then traveled by train, on the *Great Northern Railway,* and joined Oscar. They were soon married. Hilda was twenty-one years old and Oscar was thirty years old. The marriage took place in the home of Oscar's employer and wife, with the large crew of fellow carpenters in attendance. Hilda's father, Nels, and brother Olaf both came to Seattle for the wedding and also to attend the Exposition. The wedding celebration went on for three or four days and nights, another old Swedish custom.

In Seattle two children soon joined the new couple. They named their first-born, Elna Irene, and her brother born a year later, Roy. The first name, Elna, only seemed natural as both grandmothers and Mrs. Olson who raised Irene's mother, Hilda, were named Elna. But the name my mother was known by and always used was Irene.

In the early 1900s, free homesteads and the rising wheat prices attracted thousands of settlers to the vast Canadian prairie lands, known today as "Canada's Breadbasket." At that time, Hilda's father, Nels Jacobson, was still living on his homestead claim and encouraged the young couple to come. With great courage and enthusiasm, Oscar and Hilda decided to go.

Leaving Seattle, Irene was only fourteen months old and her brother, Roy, was just one month old. Both babies were too young to remember riding in the red baby buggy together, the ship or train, or the 'team and wagon' ride on their long journey to Grandpa Nels' place out on the Saskatchewan prairie. Little Irene, Roy, and their mother and father spent the first winter at Grandpa Nels' in a half-finished cabin that he was building to replace his sod house. Hilda spent most evenings removing the many slivers Irene collected from the rough-sawed lumber inside. In return for their winter stay, Oscar built Nels a nice, big barn.

When springtime came, Irene's mother and father picked out a homestead claim of their own. Oscar and Hilda filed their claim on the west half of 27-7-19, thirty-seven miles from Gull Lake, and about six miles from Grandpa Nels' place. This is where they lived until Irene was nine years old and the family returned to Seattle.

After the boundaries were located and marked with metal stakes, the homestead had to be proved up. This meant you must live on it for six months of the year and break at least ten acres of sod a year; the only exception was, if a son had a homestead he could live at his parents' house while he did his breaking and got the land ready for cropping.

Irene said her mother and father made a good team! "My mother was really the farmer in the family. She learned her farming skills in North Dakota on the Olson farm. It's a good thing because my father was no farmer. In Sweden he wasn't raised on a farm and when we first moved to the prairie, I heard he didn't even know how to put a harness on a horse! My father was a carpenter. He could build almost anything – he even made beautiful furniture!" Oscar learned his carpentry skills growing up in Sweden from his father Sven, who was a carpenter, and had a casket making business. Oscar had two older brothers, Magnus and Lars, and one younger brother named Sten (pronounced 'Stone'). His three brothers were also carpenters. ('snickare' in Swedish – 'carpenter' in English.) The youngest in the family was a sister named Justina. My mother referred to her as "Aunt Stina." Throughout their lives they corresponded and exchanged family news and photos. Stina married a wealthy government man, didn't have children, and lived in a big house with a marble stairway in Ronneby, Sweden. In a letter from Hagstad, Sweden, dated January 1, 1976, Irene's cousin, Edith, tells her, "All of us cousins live in the southern part of Skåne near the lighthouse of Sandhammar by the Baltic Sea." (The Sandhammar Lighthouse and the nearby Ale's Stones, Sweden's Stonehenge, are major tourist attractions not far from Löderup.)

The People from Skåne

Skåne (pronounced 'Skona' in Swedish) is the southern-most part of Sweden. It was once called Skåneland and was one of the three lands of Denmark. In the middle 1600s, while Sweden was at war with Russia, Poland and Austria, Denmark declared war on Sweden. Immediately Swedish forces were sent from Poland to Denmark. Denmark was defeated, which eventually required the transfers of Skåne and two other provinces to Sweden.

They say people talk funny there. They speak Swedish with a very strong accent that other Swedish people or Danish people have difficulty understanding. It's almost like a language of their own. "They say it sounds like they're speaking Swedish and Danish mixed together with a hot potato in their mouth." The Skånska dialect is soft and singing. It's said getting angry in Skånska is more efficient than in other Swedish dialects…But when spoken in a friendly voice there is nothing that sounds nicer and kinder.

3 LITTLE HOUSE ON THE CANADIAN PRAIRIE

On the vast Saskatchewan prairie where the sky and earth meet, Oscar built their little prairie house. It wasn't a "flimsy tar paper claim shanty" or a "sod house with dirt floors," like many of the homestead claims of that time. It was a small wooden house that was sturdily built and made to withstand the most severe Canadian weather. It was a snug little house with just two rooms. It had glass paned windows, a smooth wooden floor and a front door. The outside walls and the roof were both covered with hand-split cedar shingles. All of the lumber and building materials had to be hauled in by team and wagon from Gull Lake, thirty-seven miles away. There was a kitchen-dining-living room–end, all in one, and a bedroom-end. In the middle was a chimney that was shared by two stoves, back-to-back with a wall between. The bedroom-end was divided by curtains and was heated with a coal oil heater. Between the heater and the wall stood a metal fire-shield that the kids used as a blackboard. They drew pictures and wrote on it with clumps of laundry starch. The kitchen-end had a cast-iron cook stove, a long wooden table and benches handmade by Oscar, and two steamer trunks with wooden slats on top. One trunk was Oscar's and one was Hilda's. When the Rosenberg family moved from Seattle to the Saskatchewan prairie, the two trunks carried all their possessions. The trunks were also used for extra seating.

A small Swedish coffee grinder made of shiny black metal was mounted on the kitchen wall. On the bread baking days, it was used to grind the wheat they grew into a course ground graham flour. By turning the handle round and round on the hand-cranked grinder, the flour filled into a clear glass jar. Their other flour was ground at the mill. Hilda made all of the family's bread and she also made bread to sell. Her 1917 journal tells that some of the neighboring settlers were steady customers. She charged $.15 a loaf for white bread and $.20 for graham bread. The aroma of bread baking and the smells of other delicious food cooking and baking perfumed the air in the little prairie house and made it very homey inside.

On the prairie there was no electricity or running water. Coal oil lamps and lanterns brightened the nights and in the first years, the water had to be packed quite a distance in buckets from the spring at the bottom of the coulee. Later they discovered a spring that bubbled up from the ground closer to the little house that had a good water supply. Oscar dug around it and also dug a ditch that ran to the barn for the livestock to drink.

The little prairie house stood miles from anywhere. To go anywhere, they either went on foot or by horse. Leaving the farm, they traveled along their wagon trail road for quite a distance until they came to the railroad tracks of the *Canadian Pacific Railway.* Irene has fond memories of the train that traveled on those tracks. "It was the old-style steam engine with the big puffs of black smoke that billowed out of the smokestack, and at night when all of the passenger cars were lit up, we could see the people inside. The train's whistle always blew loud and a long time when it passed by our place… It seemed kind of like a familiar friend saying, 'Helllooooo! Hellooooo! Helloooo!' as it clickity clackitied along its way across the open grassland." Irene often wondered where all those people were going.

After crossing the railroad tracks, the wagon trail continued until it came to a country road. Turning left took them to Dollard. Turning right went to the Swanson's, their close friends, and then on to Shaunavon. Straight across went to Grandpa Nels', and Uncle Olaf and Aunt Emma's and the cousins' place, which was a few miles away. There were a lot of cousins! Eventually there were eleven. "In those first years when Roy and I were still very young, Mama would get so lonely she would push us two little kids in the red baby buggy all the way to Grandpa's for a visit. Then later Grandpa would bring us back with the horse and wagon."

Dollard was a very small village about four or five miles away. It had a postal service and carried a few supplies. After the farm was established, this is where Hilda would drive the horse and buggy every few days to sell her eggs, cream, and freshly churned butter and buttermilk. Along the way she'd pick up some of the neighbors' fresh farm eggs and dairy, too. On one of those deliveries, the storekeeper found a dead mouse floating in one of the neighbor ladies cream cans. The storekeeper plucked out the dead mouse and told her, "Oh, that won't hurt anybody!" Hilda was shocked that the cream wasn't refused, and shocked even more when they were both paid the same.

Shaunavon was twelve to fourteen miles away. After the new *Weyburn-Lethridge Short Line*, a branch of the Canadian Pacific Railway, reached Shaunavon in 1913, Shaunavon became a bustling boom town. This is where Oscar and Alfred Swanson built their carpentry shop. Irene said, "My father was the owner of the shop."

On the shop's false front in big bold letters it read ROSENBERG & SWANSON. The very first issue of the *Shaunavon Standard* newspaper dated Thursday, September 18, 1913 carried their ad that read:

ROSENBERG & SWANSON

Contractors and Builders

==

Estimates and Plans Furnished For All
Kinds of Construction Work.

==

Estimates Free. Our Motto is.
Satisfaction.

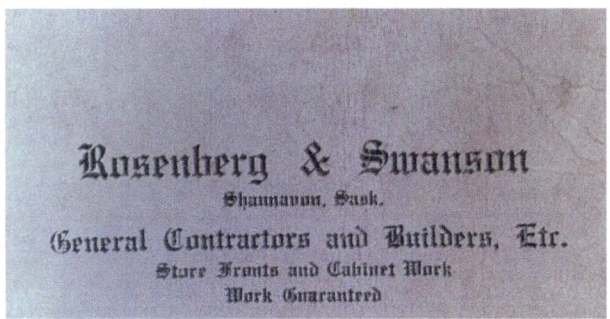

Business Card - 1913

Oscar and Alfred worked long, hard hours in building the fast-growing, frontier town. The distance was too far to ride back and forth every day, so they stayed and worked in town all week, and the women and children were left at home. The men, 'Rosenberg' and 'Swanson' as they were known, boarded the horses at the livery barn in town and rode back home to their families on the weekend. When Irene was a very young girl, she remembers going to Shaunavon by horse and buggy and seeing the *Mounties* in their red coats, riding horses there.

4   THE OXEN

When my mother was a very little girl, even before the railroad reached Shaunavon, Irene's father used a team of yoked oxen to break the prairie sod. The oxen were both the same brownish-tan color. One ox had a good straight set of horns and the other one's were crooked and twisted.

Hitched up, the oxen stood side by side and were joined by a yoke made of wood. The prairie sod wasn't deep so only a thin layer was plowed.

Irene liked to go along with her father when he was plowing and hitch a ride on the ox with the good set of horns. She'd rest her small body against the oxen's big broad head, and then reach up and hold onto his horns, Oscar would "Giddup!" the team and she'd hang on until her arms got tired. She said, "The ox didn't care, he just plugged along and plugged along while my daddy walked on behind holding the plow. When my arms got tired and I couldn't hang on anymore, Daddy would 'Whoa!' the team and I would slide down the ox's big head and play in the newly turned sod. Then Daddy would 'Giddup!' the oxen again and I would build a little sod house while they finished plowing each furrow all the way to the end. It was a long distance. They were so far away I could barely see them. When they would get back to me again, the next plowed furrow would cover over the little house I had built, and then we would repeat this process of 'Giddup! Whoa! Giddup!' Over and over…"

5 QUICKSAND

Irene said, "My mother and father were very hospitable and sociable. They had lots of friends and we always had company. Most of the prairie farmers around came to our house to get their hair cut. Everyone called my father 'Rosenberg.' He had a knack for cutting hair and he didn't charge – he just did it out of the kindness of his heart."

"Nels, a neighbor bachelor, not Grandpa Nels, would walk about three miles to get his haircut. One day he showed up completely covered with mud. He had fallen in a quicksand hole, but was able to reach a small clump of tough rooted grass that was growing on the very edge and pull himself out. Otherwise, probably no one would have ever found him forever…"

"The ox with the crooked horns also got stuck in quicksand. They used the other ox with the good set of horns to pull him out. But sadly, from all the straining and pulling, the ox with the crooked horns died from the injuries he sustained."

"Many animals and people alike fell into the quicksand and couldn't get out. The more they struggled, the deeper they went…"

6   PRAIRIE CHIPS

Prairie chips are horse and cow manure dried and bleached by the wind and sun, and as light in weight as a dry sponge.

On the timber-less plains, the 'prairie stoves' were designed to burn twisted bundles of hay, prairie chips and coal. The little house's shiny black cook stove that stood in the kitchen had four round stove lids on top. There were two lids in front and two in back, with the oven below. There was no warming oven on top.

Irene and Roy used the red folding baby buggy, that they had outgrown, to gather the prairie chips, and if they found a cow pie or horse biscuits that weren't all the way dry, they would kick them over with their shoe so they'd continue to dry in the sun and wind. They would pick them up on another day.

A good supply of prairie chips was stored in the lean-to shed beside the house to burn for fuel, as was lignite coal that they'd haul home from the mine with the team of horses and wagon. They didn't use newspaper to start the fire because it was scarce. They dried the shrubbery sticks that grew by the coulee, along with the prairie chips to get the fire started.

7   QUEENIE AND TOOTSIE

Queenie

Queenie was their faithful and very smart cattle dog. There were no fences on the prairie. All the neighboring farms grazed their cattle together to eat the prairie grasses, sometimes they would wander quite a distance away. When it was time for the cows to come home, Hilda would say, "Queenie, go get the cows!" And off she would go, all alone, and herd every one of their cattle and bring them all back to the barn.

Tootsie

Tootsie dog was a small Fox Terrier that lived in the little prairie house with the family. She was a special playmate to the kids, and at night she slept under the sheepskin coat at the kids' feet and kept them safe.

Whenever the family went somewhere, they never took Queenie or Tootsie to ride along in the wagon, buggy or sleigh. It was known that if there were wolves around, they would attack if they caught wind of a dog. Tootsie didn't like the family to leave her alone and when they left the little prairie house, she would keep herself busy by pulling off all the blankets and bedding from everyone's bed. She'd be so happy when they were back home together again.

8   STORMS

The electrical storms were severe! The lightning sizzled, the thunder rumbled and roared, and the hail flattened and ruined the crops! "The thunder cracked so loud it would shake our house and sometimes it would shake the stove lids right off the cook stove! The Tootsie dog and us kids would get so scared we'd crawl under the bed and hide until it was over. And lightning does strike twice! It struck the Swanson's little prairie house two different times. Both times their house burned to the ground! They lived with us until my father and Alfred rebuilt. And another time there was a small pond of water from the melted snow that gathered by the clothesline pole, where a wild mama duck and her baby ducks were swimming, and a flash of lightning struck the pole and blew it all to splinters and electrocuted and killed the mama duck and all of her ducklings!"

Irene especially remembers one terrible storm. "It was an early fall storm with thunder and lightning and hail and howling high winds that pounded against the bedroom window!" Hilda was afraid they would be injured if the glass broke! Irene helped her mother push the bed up against the wall and under the window. "When the strong gushes of wind and hail came, we climbed up and stood on the bed and held a heavy quilt against the glass with our bodies. Over and over, all night long we repeated this until the winds finally quieted and the storm passed. The next morning, the outside wall of our little house that had been pelted with the large hail stones looked like someone had pounded it all over with a hammer." It was those kinds of storms that ruined crop after crop – year after year! That's what the farmers called 'being hailed out!'

9   RHYMES AND RIDDLES FROM HILDA'S TRUNK

Hilda's early Rush River School reading lessons

The Ducks That Quarrreled

An old mother duck had ducklings three. And two of them could never agree. When one would go to the pond to play, the other wanted at home to stay.

From Hilda's Drawing Book.

'Twas quack, quack, quack! From morn to night. And the mother could never tell which was right. The third little duckling made no ado, but said to his mother, "I'll stay with you."

One day, as usual, these two fell out, And no one could tell what 'twas all about. They quacked so loud and made such a splash, that a fox crept up and caught them both at a dash.

The Elf Child

1.

Little Orphant Annie's come to our house to stay,
An' wash the cups an' saucers up,
an' brush the crumbs away,
An' shoo the chickens off the porch,
an' dust the hearth, an' sweep,
An' make the fire, an' bake the bread,
an' earn her board an' keep.
An' all the other children,
when the supper things is done,
We set around the kitchen – fire
an have the mostest fun,
A-list'nin to the witch tales
'at Annie tells about,
An' the gobble-uns'll gits you,
Ef you Don't Watch Out!

2.

Onct they was a little boy
Wouldn't say his pray'rs
An' when he went to bed at night,
away up stairs,
His mamma heird him holler,
an' his daddy heird him bawl,
An' when they turned the kivvers down
He wasn't there at all.
An' they seeked him in the rafter-room,
an' cubby-hole an' press,

an' seeked him up the chimbly-flue,
and everywheres, I guess.
But all they ever found was thist
His pants an' roundabout!
An' the gobble-uns'll git you
Ef you Don't Watch Out!

3.

An' one time a little girl'ud
allus laugh an' grin,
an' make fun of ever'one
an' all her blood-an' kin.
An' onct when they was "Company,"
an' ole folks was there,
she mocked 'em an' shocked 'em,
an' said she didn't care!
An' thist as she kicked her heels
an' turnt to run and hide,
they was two great big Black Things
a' standin' by her side.
An' they snatched her through the ceilin'
'fore she knowed what she's about!
An' the gobble-uns'll git you
Ef you Don't Watch Out!

4.

An little Orphant Annie says,
when the blaze is blue,
an' the lamp wick sputters,
an' the wind goes woo-oo!
An' you hear the crickets quit,
an' the moon is gray,

An' the lightnin' bugs in dew
is all squenched away,
You better mind yer parents,
an' yer teachers fond an' dear,
an' cherish them 'at loves you,
an' dry the orphant's tear,
An' help the po' needy ones
'at clus-ters all about,
Er the gobble-uns'll git you
Ef you Don't Watch Out!

Frogs at School	**Riddles or Puzzles**
Twenty froggies went to school, Down beside a rushing pool. Twenty little coats of green, Twenty vests all white and clean. "We must be in time," said they, "First we study, then we play. That is how we keep the rule, When we froggies go to school." Master froggie grave and stern, Called the classes in their turn. Taught them how to nobly strive, Likewise how to leap and dive. From his seat upon the log, Showed them how to say, "Kerchog." Also how to dodge a blow, From sticks which bad boys throw. Twenty froggies grew up fast, Big frogs they became at last. Not one lesson they forgot, Polished in a high degree, As each froggie ought to be. Now they sit on other logs, Teaching other little frogs.	1. A pack of wolves ran by. One was shot. How many remained? 2. I have four legs and feathers, But am neither beast nor bird. What am I? 3. What walks upside down overhead? 4. What are two brothers that live on opposite sides of the road yet never see each other? 5. Four brother ran side by side, but never catch one another. What are we? 6. There are four brothers under one hat. What are they? 7. People pray for me and long for my company, But directly, I appear they hide from me. What am I? 1. The dead one. 2. A feather bed. 3. A fly. 4. Your eyes. 5. Wheels of a cart. 6. Legs of a table. 7. Rain.

Robins and Pussy Willow

Two merry little builders,
Were sitting side by side.
And one was Robin Red-breast,
The other was his bride.

But gentle mistress Robin
Was filled with sudden fear.
She heard some children whisper,
"Miss Puss is very near."

She listened faint and breathless,
And wild her terror grew.
So to the skyward branches,
With throbbing heart she flew.

Her husband quickly followed,
And laughed with all his might.
He knew the funny blunder,
That caused her such a fright.

Said he, "We're miles from Catville,
And have no cause to fear.
The only pussy near us,
Is Pussy-willow-dear."

10   PRAIRIE MUSHROOMS AND WILDFLOWERS

"I will never forget that after a nice rain in the early spring, the sun would come out again and like magic would appear the beautiful, wild prairie flowers blooming everywhere and the little button mushrooms popping out of the prairie thick." (A favorite saying: "I'm a prairie flower growing wilder by the hour.")

Irene and Roy would push the red baby buggy and take along the two dogs, Queenie and Tootsie, and go pack the whole buggy almost full of the mushrooms – enough for a nice feast.

Their mother would tell them not to pick the great big ones with the black gills or the real teeny-tiny ones because they could be poisonous! "Only pick the middle-sized ones with the pink gills underneath."

When they had gathered enough mushrooms and had picked a nice bouquet of flowers for their mother, they'd push the baby buggy full of the mushrooms home for their mother to cook. Hilda would sauté them in butter with some salt and pepper. "Oh, they smelled so good cooking! We could hardly wait! That would be our whole meal, along with some of Mama's homemade bread. We just loved them!"

The following prayer was always spoken in Swedish before every meal:

Giving Thanks

Yeesa num to bords ve go

Vel sangla gud for mot

Vi fo. Awemen

(Pronounced)

In Jesus' name to the table we go

To give thanks for our food. Amen.

(English)

11 WILD STRAWBERRIES

The coulee was a shallow gully with a spring at the bottom. It was the only source of fresh water near their place for several years. In the spring, summer, and fall, Oscar and Hilda hauled their water home from the coulee in buckets. In the winter Oscar broke the ice.

For just a short while in the springtime, there were patches of wild strawberries that grew down in the coulee. My mother said, "When they were nice and ripe, they looked just like little red jewels!" She said they were very small, much smaller than a thimble with teeny-tiny seeds. They were extremely sweet and fragrant.

The little red strawberries with their small white blossoms grew all tangled and thickly matted. "Us kids would lie down on our stomachs and eat and eat them. We would keep crawling over to new spots and keep eating more and more. There were so many berries, we didn't care if the ones we laid on squished juice all over our clothes, and Mama didn't care either, because they were so good!"

"Wild strawberry season was something we looked forward to every year."

12   CHOKECHERRIES AND SASKATOONS

"In the summer we made two trips way across the prairie to pick wild fruit. First when the Saskatoons were ripe, then later when the Chokecherries were ripe. Everyone looked forward to going to the Old Pete Johnson's place where the fruit grew thick. It was also known as Preacher Johnson's coulee."

Hilda and the surrounding neighbor women would hitch up their horses to wagons and buggies and plan to make a whole day of it. In the early morning when it was still dark they loaded up the kids, took tubs and buckets, picnic lunches and some gunnysacks of hay for the horses, and headed across the prairie for Pete Johnson's. Out on the prairie, as far as your eye could see in every direction, everything was flat except for the low-rolling foothills of the Cypress Hills where they went to pick the fruit. "It didn't look far but it was a long, long way. We had to ride for hours to get there and we had to ride for hours to get back home. We left at the 'crack of dawn' and returned sometime before dark with the tubs and buckets brimful."

"We didn't know Pete Johnson, no one knew him. No one lived at his place. It was an abandoned and weather-beaten old farmstead that had been vacant for many years. The old farmhouse had a lot of rooms and when we hollered it echoed inside. It was mysterious that no one lived there. There was even a barn where we could put the horses to rest and eat. Us kids had lots of fun playing and exploring all over while the mothers were picking. At lunchtime everyone picnicked inside the old house."

"The next day and the next day, our little prairie house smelled sooo good – Mama slowly cooked down all the fruit with some sugar and made a good supply of delicious syrup for our pancakes and cornbread."

13 UP TO NO GOOD

"In all the seasons we went to sleep listening to the wind and owls and the coyotes yipping and howling until the early morning."

Sometime in the darkness of the night, when Hilda and the children were asleep in bed, they were awakened by the sounds of their geese honking in terror! The gander was honking the loudest! These terrifying honks went on for hours and the gander didn't stop until the early morning. Oscar was working and staying in town. There wasn't anything they could do but wait and listen in agony. Hilda didn't shoot a gun and it was too dark and dangerous to go outside.

When daylight finally came enough to see, and they felt safe to go outside to look, "There we saw our whole flock of about a dozen geese with bloody feathers all dead, strewn all over, even the gander. It could have been wolves or a fox and her kits, but we always blamed the coyotes! Whatever killed them wasn't hungry but had been out for a night of sport."

Guns

Irene said her father had two guns, a pistol and a shotgun. The gun that Oscar always brought in the sleigh and buggy was one he found in a restaurant. It was a deluxe model revolver that once belonged to a Canadian Mountie. The shotgun had a single-barrel and was used to hunt small wild game. Oscar kept a steady supply of cottontail rabbits, prairie chickens and ducks for the table.

14 THE GOOSEBONE

Goosebone, goosebone, please tell me
How cold will this winter be?
Will it be one mild, or rough?
Will you give us snow enough?
Will a zero temperature make us burn
our furniture?
Or instead, will open work be in style
where frost should lurk?
Will the fat man slip and slide on the ice
and fall, like pride?
Will we have a backward spring?
Will we hear the sleigh bells ring?
Will we have a yuletide white?
Will we have one clear and bright?
Will the ground freeze very deep?
Will the price of coal be steep?
Goosebone, goosebone, please tell me
How cold will this winter be?

Poem: From Hilda's trunk
Rush River School lesson

15 THE BLIZZARD

One cold and crisp winter morning with a snow-covered ground and a clear, blue sky, Hilda took the long trip into Shaunavon while the children stayed at home with their father. She took the one-horse sleigh and Lightfoot, their fastest and most spirited buggy horse. Hilda would have to go all the way to Shaunavon to get the supplies she couldn't get in Dollard. Dollard was a closer little village where she sold her eggs, butter and cream, but it was just a spot on the road.

On the prairie, the clear winter sky can suddenly blow up into a dangerous blizzard. While Hilda was in town, the sky grew dark and threatening and the winds were picking up. She hurriedly left for home. The blizzard came faster than they could drive and caught them out on the prairie. Blinded by the swirling, stinging snow Hilda couldn't even see the tail end of Lightfoot just a few feet in front of her and she couldn't tell which way was home. It was a whiteout! She grew up knowing the danger! They could lose their way and freeze to death as many others had! Remembering what she had learned as a girl, Hilda realized her only choice was to completely trust the horse to find his way. She gave him free rein and tied up the reins on the dash holder. Shouting through the biting snow and howling wind, she commanded him saying, "Giddup! C'mon! Take us home!"

Hilda crawled down on the floorboards of the sleigh and pulled the sleigh blanket around her and over her head. With the blinding snow blowing and coming from all directions, she hoped and prayed the horse could find the only place where he could safely cross the railroad tracks without upsetting the sleigh. Lightfoot pulled the sleigh on…and on…and on…until they came to a dead stop. Fearfully, Hilda looked out from under the icy, snow covered blanket. She was afraid the horse had just stalled and they were truly lost, but as she lifted the blanket, she saw instead that Lightfoot had found his way home and had pulled the sleigh right up to the door of their little prairie house.

Irene remembers that day, anxiously waiting and listening by the window for her mother and Lightfoot. "It was snowing so hard outside the air was white! Oh! How excited and relieved we were when suddenly, we heard the familiar sounds of the horse 'n sleigh and Mama's voice outside!"

16 WINTER

Oscar and Alfred didn't go to the carpentry shop in Shaunavon to work during the coldest winter months. School was closed starting late in December, after the big Christmas program, when the snow started to pile up. It didn't open again until the warm Chinook wind came and melted all the snow in the early spring.

"Sometimes the snow got so deep it came way up to the rooftop and we couldn't even see out of the windows!" Snow steps climbed upward from the door to the top of the snow outside, and as the snow grew deeper another step was added. But their little prairie house was built good and strong and kept them safe and warm inside. The snow outside got so frozen they could walk on top of it and so could the horses without sinking down.

The barn and chicken house were cozy warm too – kept bedded deep with straw so the animals could keep their own warmth inside and not freeze to death. The chicken house was built on top of the barn, and during those cold winter months a rope was strung between the house and barn. In a white-out blizzard when they couldn't even see the barn, they could hang on to the rope and find their way back and forth to milk the cows and feed and care for the cattle, horses, chickens, ducks, geese and turkeys. There was an overhang built on the side of the barn where they parked the horse wagon, sleighs and buggy, which kept them from getting buried under the deep snow.

Oscar went to the spring and broke the ice to melt for their drinking water. They also collected the new snow that fell on the frozen snow steps in a big dishpan to melt on top of the cook stove. The melted snow water was used for washing the dishes, the clothes and for their baths. "Mama washed all our clothes by hand on a scrub board, and she ironed them with heavy flat irons that she heated on top of the cook stove."

Hilda raised a pig every year and Oscar and Grandpa Nels butchered it when the weather was cold enough so it could hang outside all winter and stay frozen. When they wanted some, Oscar would just go out and saw off a chunk. Nothing was wasted; even the pig's head was shaved, cleaned and cooked and made into loaves of headcheese. The lard was rendered, and some was used for cooking but most was sold in Dollard. The special fluffy hog lard was saved for a special treat or when the butter supply was low, Adolf remembered, "We liked to spread it on Mama's warm fresh baked bread. We sprinkled it with a little bit of salt and pepper… it was really good!"

Before the snow fell, the kids had lots of fun on their lake-sized pond when it froze over. Irene doesn't know if her father made up his own plan or if it was something they used in Sweden. He made them foot sleds. They were made of wood and were quite short in length, only about a foot or a little longer. They curved up in the front like a regular sled and had leather straps to put their feet in. Oscar used the metal hoops that held the nail-kegs together on the bottom of the sled runners. He pounded a good-sized nail part way into the end of a long pole and filed off the nail head, leaving a sharp point. This was the push off pole.

"We would straddle the pole like riding on a child's hobbyhorse stick toy with the spike-end sticking in the ice behind us. We could also steer with the pole. To get moving, we'd have to push off with the pole and use our arms to keep pushing off and pushing off."

…And then when the really big winter snow came and the snow drifts were piled up all around them, even when the wind was howling, and it was snowing hard, and everything was white and frozen, Irene said that 'Santa Claus' still could find their little prairie house for Christmas. "In our beds at night us kids could hear the sleigh bells coming!"

A Week of Winter

January

Mon	29	sunshine but very cold all day
Tues	30	very cold & snow drifting a little, the coldest we have had
Wed	31	very cold, sunshine 50 below zero

February

Thurs	1	very cold & sunshine & clear
Fri	2	clear and a little milder, snow drifting
Sat	3	snowstorm all day, snow drifting, our ox died in the night
Sun	4	windy all day, snow drifting

- Hilda's Journal 1917

The following drawings from Hilda's Drawing book at Rush River School.

Cover

The Anders Olson Farm where Hilda grew up.

17   APPLE PEELINGS

At Christmastime, Grandpa Nels always ordered a small wooden barrel of apples that would come on the train to Shaunavon. Nels gave each family of friends and relatives about a dozen as a gift. The kids couldn't just eat the whole apples fresh. They were saved special for the apple pie their mother made for their Christmas dessert. On the pie-baking day, Hilda always made a little more piecrust dough for them. She rolled it out, brushed it lightly with butter or some milk, and sprinkled it with sugar and some ground cinnamon. She then cut out fancy shapes and baked them. Some she cut in diamonds and some she cut in strips. Some of the strips she twisted and some she rolled up like a jellyroll. When they came out of the oven the kids had a delicious feast of piecrust and the apple peelings. Then for Christmas the three little kids each would find in their Christmas stocking a whole juicy apple all polished and shiny, just for them.

Irene, Roy and Adolf never tasted any other fruit except what grew wild on the prairie and the rhubarb that grew in their own garden.

Irene remembers eating her first orange when they moved back to Seattle when she was nine years old. "At that time, I didn't even know what an orange or banana was."

Apple Pie

Peel & slice very thin apples, enough to fill a pie tin.
Line pan with crust.
Put in the apples.
Cover with sugar & ground cinnamon.
Cover with crust.
Bake
            - Hilda

18 WOLVES

Saskatchewan in the winter was a lonesome wilderness. Sometimes temperatures reached fifty degrees below zero. The frozen barren land made living harsh for the settlers, but the family didn't stay house bound. They went out to visit the different neighbors and to Grandpa and Uncle Olaf and Aunt Emma and the cousin's, just as they did the rest of the year.

When enough snow covered the ground, Oscar turned their buggies into sleighs by taking off the wheels and putting the sled runners on. The two-horse open sleigh was pulled by their buggy team, Lightfoot and Fanny. "Our sleigh was a real fancy, deluxe model. We felt pretty ritzy when Lightfoot 'n Fanny were all hitched up with their sleigh bells on and we were all ready to go!" The sleigh had a curved dash in the front, it was partly closed on the sides and was open at the end. Little Adolf sat up in the front on their mother's lap, beside their father. Irene and Roy rode in the open back part and they curled up together inside their father's long sheepskin coat. "We brought along heated rocks from the cook stove's oven wrapped in gunnysacks and old blankets to help keep us warm. The rocks were flat and oval but too heavy for us kids to carry. When we reached the neighbors' or Grandpa's house the rocks were put in their oven so they would have time to reheat for the return trip. The rocks would still be warm enough to put in our own bed when we got back home."

When the family rode across the prairie, they were exposed to whatever nature had in store. Sometimes large packs of wolves followed them in the moonlit darkness. "Roy and I would be snuggled way under the fleece-lined coat hiding and trying to stay warm and we could hear our mother and father talking in Swedish about seeing the wolves or the wolves following us! One time a whole pack of at least ten to twelve kept working their way closer and closer to the open-end of our sleigh until they were only a few feet away! We could hear them, they made eerie noises! They didn't howl but made sounds like whining and a snarling growl-yip! They came so close that we could see their breath in the moonlight! After a while we dared to peek out into the bitter cold to see if they were still there. Our father would tell us in Swedish, 'Never mind, Daddy will take care of you!' We knew he was a good shot and he always brought his gun in case we should meet danger. But the wolves never did attack the horses or us, and our father never had to use his gun. The wolves would suddenly leave, just as they suddenly appeared. We figured they were just curious about us as we were traveling through."

19   A COUNTRY GIRL

Oh! What is so free and joyful
What is so healthful and bright
What is so gladsome and happy
As our country lassie's life.

No slave of Dame Fashion is she,
She can laugh at society's whims,
Propriety in the country is not so stern
Yet in the city are many more sins.

Think of her city cousin so trim,
With her hair all puffs and curls,
With her Paris dress of satin and lace
Her waist bedecked with pearls.

What would she do in a farmyard,
With her milk pail on her arm,
If she were suddenly transplanted,
From the ballroom to the farm?

And the little country lassie
Will make the best woman, I know
True, kind-hearted, industrious,
She will make her way where 'er
She may go.

If she and her city cousin,
Were thrown side by side, to
Work and make their living

In the world so big and wide,

Which do you think would be the first
To deserve and achieve renown,
The country lassie so modest and shy
Or her pretty cousin from town?

**1904 Poem from Hilda's Trunk
Rush River School lesson**

20 THE BASKET SOCIAL BARN DANCES

The popular school fundraisers at that time were the Basket Socials. They were a fun and joyful night for the whole family, filled with lots of food, toe-tapping music, lively dancing and a fundraising auction. There would always be a large turnout and a successful auction sale.

The Basket Socials would be held in one of the areas' largest barns. The neighboring farmers, along with their wives and kids and young singles alike, all looked forward to the upcoming event. On the night of the Big Barn Dance, the ladies would bring along a beautifully prepared 'Dessert Basket' that would be auctioned off later in the night. And after an evening of socializing and energetic dancing and the night grew late, the kids were bedded down in the big stacks of hay that were piled around the edges of the dancing area. The adults danced on into the night to the music of the fiddler, or someone's accordion.

Sometime before the midnight hour the auction would begin. The big barn would be all darkened except for the stage area where a white sheet would be hung up with bright lantern light shining from behind. Each lady would take her turn behind the sheet. The lantern light would cast her shadow onto the sheet in view of the gentlemen gathered around. The men would whistle and holler and bid back and forth as the auctioneer cried out the bids. One by one the shadow ladies would appear with her basket and try to outbid one another. They were very competitive! In her turn, each lady would pose or do a little dance; maybe a little can-can leg kick or something else a bit more risqué, all in the spirit of the night, and in the hopes of getting a higher bid. The highest bidder would then have the honor of dancing with the lady, and sharing her basket's specialty. Irene remembered, "The bigger kids would go peek and we'd try to guess who the shadows were. It looked like some of the shadow ladies took off some of their clothes, and some even got all naked...!" After the auction intermission, the dancing resumed and the adults 'kicked up their heels' until the wee morning hours.

When Lightfoot 'n Fanny brought the family back to their little prairie house, the sun would be coming up, the meadowlarks were singing, the rooster was crowing, and it was almost time to milk the cows. "Oh! Those were fun times on the prairie!"

21   THE ONE-ROOM PRAIRIE SCHOOL

Irene couldn't wait until her brother, Roy, was old enough to go to school. When Roy turned six years old and Irene was seven, they both started school in the first grade together. "I dressed up in a dress every day at home and every day to go to school — I didn't even own a pair of pants and Roy always wore knee-pants and long, dark knee socks. Our mother and father were very fussy about our appearance and manners. Mama ordered most of our clothes from the *Eaton's* catalogue which was delivered by train to Shaunavon."

'Avon Heights' (pronounced avv'en) was a brand new one-room country school out on the open prairie with a total of fifteen or sixteen pupils. "My father helped build the schoolhouse and the horses' shed." Hilda and Oscar were both active in the school's affairs, and Oscar was a member of the first school board. Irene and Roy started school in Avon Heights' second year.

A large cast-iron heater that burned coal kept the little prairie school nice and warm. In those days there was no electricity or running water. There was window-light and the water supply was in a tin bucket with a dipper that sat on a wooden bench. A shelf on the wall nearby held each of the pupil's drinking cups that they brought from home. A path outdoors led to the outside toilets.

Sometimes Irene and Roy walked to school and sometimes they rode double on Lady, Irene's horse. "Lady was a beautiful, red-brown color and in the middle of her forehead she had a small white star. I loved my Lady horse who was a darling friend in every way except she was very skittish! She was even scared of her own shadow. If something spooked her, you'd better hang on tight 'cause she'd start dancing and prancing and hopping around and act like she was ready to take off for the moon! The schoolhouse was about a mile and a half away. It was just across the coulee and a little way more. We brought our lunches to school in a tin lard pail, and we brought enough feed for Lady in a gunnysack."

All summer long the wild roses bloomed with beautiful, fragrant, pink flowers… and in the autumn, their bright red and orange clusters of rose hips would be ripe. "Roy and I liked to pick handfuls here and there to eat along the way to and from school. They were kinda tangy tasting and soooo good! Some were as big as marbles."

Winter was a dangerous time to travel for the pioneer families. The school year was only about six months long, so the kids worked extra hard all day at the school to keep ahead in their grade.

Miss McNaught was their teacher and she taught all eight grades. Some of the grades were empty or with only one or two pupils. Each pupil had their own desk and a primer lesson book, which they kept from year to year. There was no writing paper or pencils; instead each pupil was given a slate in a wooden frame, a slate-pencil and a slate-rag to use.

The first thing every morning, even before they had a piano, the new little school's day started by singing 'O Canada,' which is today Canada's national anthem. Throughout the day the kids would come up individually, or in groups, to the long wooden bench in front of the teacher's desk to recite, answer questions or listen to a lesson. Anyone who finished their assignments would be given more work at the blackboard.

"Us kids all ate our lunches together at our school desks. After lunch we were free to go outside and play for recess. There wasn't too much to do outside. Sometimes we played games, or we went to the horse shed and brushed and petted the horses — sometimes we rode them around. When school was dismissed at the end of the day, the kids would have to clean up the horse piles in the horse shed before they left for the ride home."

Some of the pupils were already young men, fourteen to sixteen years old, but still in the lower grades. They didn't have much spare time to attend school because their help was needed to work on their family's farm.

"Once, while we were at school there was a big prairie fire that was heading straight towards us! The story was… A berry picker had cooked some dinner and hadn't put out the campfire completely. The winds fanned up the fire and it caught the neighbor's haystack on fire! It continued to spread! We could see lots of smoke and flames coming!

There was a breaking around the school, but not enough to stop it! Roy and I got Lady out of the horse shed but we didn't know what to do! Miss McNaught had the kids go out on the breaking and stay with the horses. The big boys went out with wet sacks. And all the prairie farmers could also see the smoke and fire, and they came with horses and plows and lit a back-fire and got it out."

One year the school kids planted potatoes on the breaking and it was a very good crop. That year the price of potatoes went sky high. The money the kids raised from the potato sale bought a lot of playground equipment for their schoolyard.

When Irene and Roy left the prairie, they were in the third grade. When they started school in Seattle at the big B.F. Day School, they found that they were way ahead of the other kids in their same grade, so they were put ahead into the fifth grade.

22 FREEHAND PAPER CUTTING CONTEST
Little Red Hen

Irene's artistic talent showed up at a very early age. Even with the lack of art supplies, Irene found one way to express her creativity.

Using a pair of scissors, she loved to do freehand paper cut-outs. "My mother saved every little scrap piece of paper she could find for me – wrapping paper and sometimes she gave me the 'Shaunavon Standard' newspaper to cut." Irene could spend hours sitting under the prairie sky cutting out all the familiar silhouettes she knew. Oxen, cows, horses and mules, prairie chickens, wolves, foxes and coyotes, dogs, cats and mice, chickens, turkeys, pigs, ducks, rabbits, geese and owls. On a blank piece of paper she would imagine the image that she wanted to cut, and without any lines to follow, she usually started cutting just in front of the tail on the rump-end – cutting along the back, up the neck, around the head and down the legs. Horses were her favorite.

When Irene was in the second grade her teacher, Miss McNaught, entered her cut-outs in an art contest. Contestants from 150 prairie schools in Canada participated. The theme of her entry was 'Little Red Hen.' Irene won first prize and received two large red satin ribbons that awarded First Prize and $5.00 in money! Her mother and father were very proud and so was she! In Canada, red ribbons are First Prize and blue ribbons are Second Prize.

23 GYPSIES

Irene and Roy loved going to school, and they loved their teacher. After school they liked to stay and help her. Miss McNaught would put them to work sweeping or cleaning the blackboards, and things like that.

One day, when they were only in the first or second grade and had just started the walk for home and were close by the coulee, they heard the clomping of horse hooves and the squeaking and rattling of wagon wheels approaching. There they saw a large band of gypsies in covered wagons that were traveling through. No one had ever warned them that gypsies were nomads and wanderers and often stole things, even children! Irene and Roy curiously watched each wagon as it passed by. On the very last rig that passed they saw a lone gypsy man sitting on the tail end of the wagon bed! He spotted them and motioned and hollered for them to come over, saying, "Hey kids! Kids! Come on, come on and go for a ride! We've got lots of kids, you will be so happy! Come on!" The gypsy man then jumped down from his perch that stuck out from the back of the wagon and ran towards them! Irene thought fast and told Roy, "Come on! Let's run back to school!" They hoped Miss McNaught hadn't left on her horse yet and would still be there. They ran like the wind, and the gypsy man chased after them. But they ran much faster than he could, so he finally stopped.

Safely back at the schoolhouse with their teacher, Irene and Roy watched the gypsy caravan rolling across the open prairie and fading away into the distance. Now far away and looking like a little speck, they could see the gypsy man running and running and trying to catch up with the wagons before they left him behind with nowhere to go.

24 GOPHER TAILS

Pioneer children were exposed to the 'raw and harsh ways of survival' from a very young age.

"On the prairie in Canada we were overrun with pocket gophers. They were so thick and were doing so much damage to the wheat crops that the school kids had to help by trapping them. They lived in long underground tunnels and there were gopher holes everywhere. They're a little bit bigger than a squirrel but they don't have a bushy tail. They're kind of a brownish color, and they have big yellow teeth, and long claws on their front feet."

"To help solve the problem, all the prairie schools around were supplied with gopher traps. The teacher passed out one trap to each pupil. The municipality paid a cent a tail bounty and it was a way for the school kids to make some spending money."

Irene said, "Every morning Roy and I set our traps on the way to school. We'd put our traps right in front of a gopher hole. That way we could catch one either way, going to its hole or leaving. We tied a pretty long stick to the trap so the gopher couldn't get away with our trap and drag it down in its hole. On the way home from school, we'd be anxious to check our traps to see if we had caught any. If we did, we'd reset our traps and in the morning we'd bring the tails to school with us and line them up on our school desks. Miss McNaught would come around the room to take count and keep track. Sometimes we'd catch one in the morning and one in the evening. Some of the kids tried to fool the teacher by making two tails out of one big one, but Miss McNaught could always tell."

25   WORLD WAR 1 FLU

"War is over, bells and whistles going for three hours at Shaunavon. Cloudy and mild. O at Albert Barclay's working. I and children were at Neste's."

- Hilda's Journal Nov. 7, 1918

On November 7, the world received a premature news story that the Germans had signed an armistice. The Armistice was signed four days later on November 11, 1918, ending World War I.

During the time they lived on the prairie, one of the worst worldwide pandemics of influenza occurred after the war in the years 1918-1919. It was also known as the Spanish Flu or the World War I Flu. Sometimes whole families would be found dead in their homes. Throughout the world millions of people died, and in Sweden, Oscar's mother, Elna, who was the children's grandmother, lost her life from this terrible flu. Swedish records show she died in 1919 at the age of 69. Her father's name was Lars, and her mother's name was Elsa, and she had 17 siblings. (Elna Larsdotter is her Swedish name.) The word passed down is that Elna was very artistic and did beautiful loom-work.

And the flu came to the prairie! Oscar and Roy contracted it, but Hilda, Irene and Adolf didn't. During their severe illness, Irene helped care for her little brother, Adolf, because her mother had all the outside chores to do alone and to care for the sick. The neighbor bachelor, Nels, came with a pint of whiskey, the medicine of that time, and told Oscar to drink it and cover up with everything, the sheepskin coat and blankets and to sweat it off. Oscar did what he was told and the next morning he was better – the fever was gone.

During his recovery, Oscar sanded and polished the ox's horns smooth from their ox with the good set of horns that had died in the fifty below winter weather the year before. He mounted them on a plaque of wood covered with a piece of burgundy velvet from Hilda's wedding dress that she had taken from her trunk.

26 GOODBYE PRAIRIE

Irene remembers the day her father came home with the big news, "Hilda! I sold the shop and the farm and we're moving back to Seattle!" After hearing the news, she remembers her mother throwing her arms in the air and jumping for joy and through the tears saying, "That's the best news I've ever heard!" At this time Hilda was expecting her fourth child, and the young pioneer wife and mother had grown tired of the remote and harsh prairie life in Canada and longed to move back to Seattle.

Oscar's former employer, Anton Lindberg, who owned the American Portable Housing Company, had written many letters to her father always wanting him to move back to Seattle to work for him again, saying he could never find another carpenter with his skills that could replace him. He offered Oscar a good wage of $9.00 a day. The average man's pay, at that time was $3.00, so it was a very good offer. After only one good wheat crop in eight years and the rest ruined by hailstorms, along with the hardships of pioneer living, Oscar and Hilda were both ready to move back to Seattle with their family for a new lifestyle. It was time to say goodbye to pioneer life, goodbye to their friends and relatives, and goodbye to their little house on the Saskatchewan prairie. The prairie stories and memories would last a lifetime.

27 THE SOD HOUSE AND BARN OWL

After selling the homestead farm and the carpentry shop in Shaunavon, Oscar went ahead of the family on the train, and then by ship, bound for Seattle to find a place for the family to live and to start his work.

Hilda and the children stayed behind and lived about a month in a vacant sod house near their Grandpa Nels' place. During this time, they attended their cousin's little prairie school. Irene and Roy were in the third grade and Adolf hadn't started school yet.

Word got around to the surrounding homesteaders about the family moving away and about the sale. The farmers came, some with teams and wagons from many miles away to buy their things. Hilda traveled with Lady and the buggy, back and forth, from the sod house to the farmstead selling all their belongings for whatever price she could get. She only kept what she could pack in her trunk. "There wasn't even room for my beautiful doll with the China head and soft leather body, I had to give her away to the neighbor girl."

Irene remembers living in the 'soddy' that had dirt floors… "The floors were shiny-smooth and hard, and you could sweep them just fine, but the one bad thing about the sod house, there were terrible bed bugs that lived in the walls! In the night, they bit us, and we would cry."

"A beautiful white barn owl lived in the big barn there, and during the daylight hours we could pet the owl. Inside the barn there was also a nice swing, with a wooden seat and long ropes attached to the beam overhead, that we would swing on. I liked to swing high and sing to the owl. The song I sang was called 'K-K-K-Katy.' "

K-K-K-Katy

K-K-K-Katy, beautiful Katy,
You're the only g-g-g-girl that I adore;
When the m-m-m-moon shines,
Over the c-c-c-cowshed,
I'll be waiting at the k-k-k-kitchen door.

World War I song, Refrain

28 THE LONG JOURNEY TO SEATTLE

"All aboard!" The steam engine roared! The bells rang! The whistle blew! And the train pulled away…

"It was in the late fall, before the snow came, when we boarded the train in Shaunavon and left the prairie. I was nine years old. I was very excited but sad all at the same time."

Remembering, Irene said her mother wasn't feeling well the whole way to Seattle. She said a male passenger helped keep Adolf and Roy entertained by hiding peanuts in the cracks of the train seats and rolling grapes down the aisle to them. Irene and Roy had free reign to the open-air car outside.

"Suddenly, we came upon a 'large herd of buffalo' that were right by the railroad tracks, so Roy and I hurried outside to look! The train slowed way down, and the whistle blew and blew, and as the train passed, we got to see the buffalo up close for the first time. That was exciting!"

"Sometimes, from our little prairie house, when the weather was dry, we'd see way off in the distance a big cloud of dust rising with about twenty to thirty head of buffalo running across the prairie, but we never got to see them up close. We'd first see the dust cloud – and there were some 'old buffalo wallows' right by our schoolhouse."

The next big thrill on their journey was traveling through the beautiful *Canadian Rockies*, and seeing the 'breathtaking views' of steeeep snow-capped mountains, trees, and lakes, and deeeep, deep canyons!

And the next, was boarding the *SS Princess Victoria* ship in Vancouver, British Columbia and 'sailing on the water' to Seattle.

The beautiful 'SS Princess Victoria' steamship was owned by the Canadian Pacific Railway. It had a steady route between Seattle, Victoria and Vancouver. It was a luxury ocean liner 300 feet long, and about 40 feet wide, with three smokestacks.

The ship arrived in Seattle on 'Armistice Day, 1919.' President

Woodrow Wilson had proclaimed November 11th as a national holiday, and Seattle was celebrating the first Armistice Day after the ending of World War I. "The roses were still blooming in the people's yards! They were beautiful! The streets were alive with festivities and celebration – Banners and flags! Marching bands! Crowds and noise! Cars and 'ooga-ooga' horns!" My mother said coming from the prairie to the city was as different as night and day! She said, "It was overwhelming!"

After arriving in Seattle, the family stayed at a hotel for a few days, then moved to a rental for a short while until they moved to their new house located in the Fremont district, close to *Woodland Park Zoo*. "Our house was close enough to 'Woodland Park' that we could walk, and when the weather was still, we could 'hear the lions roaring' at feeding time!"

The real estate contract for the purchase of their Seattle house and two lots at 726 North 43rd Street, was signed on November 17, 1919. The price was $2,300.00 with a down payment of $75.00 and payments of $25.00 or more every month. The interest rate was 7%.

"Oh! We were just thrilled with our new house! It was a nice, big house equipped with all the modern conveniences for that time. It was so exciting to have electricity and indoor plumbing — it was just like magic to switch the lights on and off and to have hot or cold running water!" My mother said it had a beautiful wooden stairway that led to the upstairs, and a good-sized covered porch at the front entrance. Every Saturday morning it was her chore to dust and polish the stairway and piano, then practice her piano lesson for one whole hour before she could go play. All the days of her life, my mother cherished and kept her piano.

When winter was over, there was yet another big thrill and more excitement when springtime came – a little sister named Violet joined their family! The year was 1920. Irene loved to help with her care, she was almost like a second mother or her nanny. Before Violet was born, their father purchased a deluxe model baby buggy. With the buggy Irene could park it close by and watch over her. As soon as Violet was big enough, she brought her right along in the buggy when she joined her friends in play. The two sisters remained close their entire life.

Irene said, 'The B.F. Day School,' just a couple blocks away, was 'castle-sized' compared to their little one-room country school with fifteen or sixteen kids. The huge school had four main entrances, one each on the north, south, east and west sides of the building, with twenty-four classrooms and about a thousand school kids. At that time the B.F. Day School was the largest grade school in Seattle.

Irene's artistic talent didn't go unnoticed. She made a charcoal drawing at school of her Grandpa Nels from memory that was selected and sent to a prestigious museum in New York for display.

My mother said they missed all their friends and relatives on the prairie, but they wrote lots of letters and sent pictures. "Almost every year, tucked in one of the letters, was a birth announcement of another cousin! Uncle Olaf and Aunt Emma sent us a fun picture with all our cousins lined up like a 'choo choo train,' one behind the other. Starting with the youngest, each one was a head taller. They looked just like a stairway with eleven steps." She said they were mostly all girls with only a couple boys. Ten had platinum blonde hair and only one girl had dark hair.

All day long the streetcar traveled back and forth and back and forth from town to Woodland Park. Before they had a car, a *Model T* Ford, Oscar caught it for work in the mornings on its way to town and home from work on its way back to Woodland Park. Irene liked to go meet the streetcar when her father came home from work. He always had a treat saved in his lunch box.

In those days there were still some horse-drawn delivery wagons making their rounds. Mom said the big blocks of ice for their ice box and the milkman both came around by horse and wagon, and farmers would come through her neighborhood with horses pulling farm wagons loaded up with seasonal fruit 'n berries and vegetables for sale.

When the pony rides first opened at Woodland Park, Irene got a job working there. Remembering her prairie life, she loved to groom, saddle up and care for the ponies and help with the rides. She exchanged working for free pony rides.

There were lots of neighborhood kids with always something fun going on. "We liked to ride bicycles, roller skate, jump rope, and play sidewalk games, jacks, cards and dress-up. The boys liked to play ball and marbles. Roy especially liked to play baseball." Irene and her dearest neighborhood friend, Flora, could spend hours on the front porch making paper-doll ladies and designing their clothes, "We were always together. We rode the streetcar, we rode the ponies, we walked to school, and Woodland Park — sometimes we'd roller skate all the way to the little grocery store. For five cents we could buy a 'big juicy pickle' out of a wooden barrel, or pick out a 'sack of penny candy,' and then roller skate all the way back again."

"It was a wonderful neighborhood!" Never forgetting her beloved prairie, my mother said Seattle was also an unforgettable place to call home.

29   THE ROCK CHILDREN

Once upon a time, a long time ago, when my mother was still a little girl on the prairie, there was a pretty good-sized hill that had a lot of rocks behind the Swanson's place. "Us kids liked to climb up that hill and look for little broken pieces of old dishes. There were all different kinds - some of the pieces had beautiful painted flowers. The mystery of how they got there was something no one knew." The Swansons built their little prairie house at the base of this hill thinking it would be a good windbreak.

For something fun to do while visiting at their friends' house, the four little children, Irene and Roy, and the Swanson children, Evelyn and Wilfred, gathered potato-sized rocks and made a big pile right up on the top. Then they all lay down on their backs with their heads closest to the rock pile in the center. When the four children joined hands, it formed an enclosed circle of two little boys in trousers and two little girls in dresses, opposite each other, looking just like the sails on an old-fashioned windmill. From the pile of gathered rocks, Irene, who was the oldest, outlined all three of their bodies with the rocks, then she lay down and Roy placed rocks around her. One larger rock was placed where their two hands met, and they placed two larger rocks for their feet.

And many years later, when Irene was a grown-up lady, and was married, and had children of her own, she returned to the place of her childhood on the Saskatchewan prairie. There, she found the little prairie house and her school…but now they were weathered and empty and all boarded up. Next she went to the Swanson's hill. And once again climbing up to the top of that same pretty good-sized hill, Irene found the rock outlines of the four little children still frolicking there – untouched by the seasons of time…

Sheaves of Wheat

Olaf and Grandpa Nels and the cousins.

30 PHOTOS FROM THE PRAIRIE GIRL STORIES (AND BEYOND)

Hilda, Irene, and Oscar

Nils Jacobsson (Hilda's Father)   Peter Jacobsson (Nils' brother)

Olaf, Hilda, and Ada Jacobsson

Fränninge Parish, Sweden. Family History & Jacobsson Genealogy records.

Mr. & Mrs. Anders Olson & Family. These are the people who raised Hilda until age 15. (*No family relation.*)

The Anders Olson farmhouse and barnyard
where Hilda grew up near Argusville, North Dakota.

Hilda's one-room schoolhouse in
Argusville, North Dakota

Hilda's Rush River Souvenirs

Rush River School House No. 63
Rush River Township
Cass County, North Dakota

The widower, his daughter Ida, and the horse, Prince.

Oscar's employer, Anton Lindberg and family at Exposition in Seattle 1909.

Hilda. Her blouse cost a whole months pay at the boarding house.

Written on back: "Miss Hilda Nelson, age 17, 1907. I am working in Fargo, N.D."

RMS Carmania 1907. Oscar's ship to America.

Oscar's ship embarked from Liverpool -1907.

Inspection Card - Ellis Island Manifest sheet.

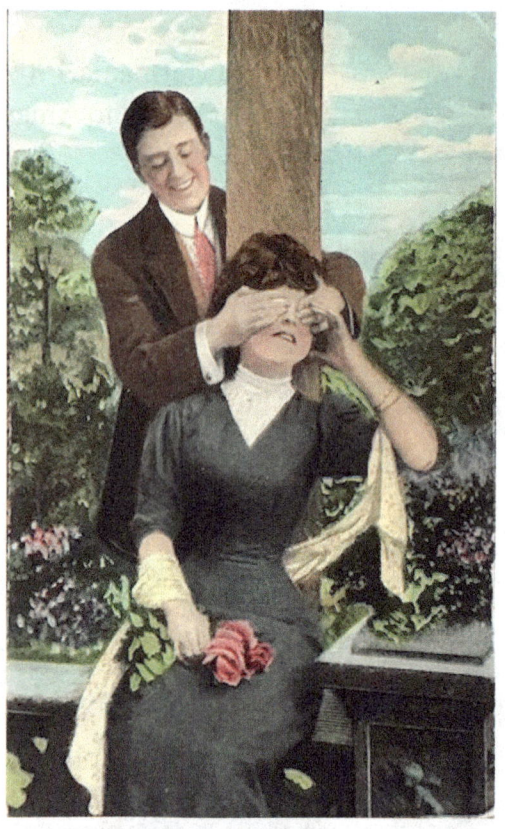

Addressed to Hilda Nelson (at Boarding House) in North Dakota. Post marked Lumber Camp #2, Deer River, Minnesota with the initials O.G.R. only.

Courting Days for Hilda and Oscar. Postcards were written in Swedish. 1907

Oscar George Rosenberg
Irene's Father.

Seattle, Washington 1908.
Postcard from Oscar to Hilda.

1909 Alaska-Yukon-
Pacific
Exposition Postcard
Seattle, Washington

Postcards from
Oscar to Hilda

1909 Alaska - Yukon- Pacific
Exposition Postcard.
'Mount Rainier'

Löderup Parish, Sweden. Family History & Rosenberg Genealogy records.

Elna Larsdotter Rosenberg and Sven Mansson Rosenberg - Oscar's parents in Sweden.

Löderup 27, Sweden. (Oscar's parents' brickhous Sitting: Sven and Elna. Brother & sister: Sten & Justina.

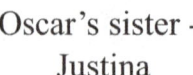

Oscar

Oscar's sister - Justina

Irene's Birth Announcement.
Delivered August 16, 1910. Weight: 9 lbs.
Received 9:00 a.m. c.o.d. O.Rosenberg

Irene, Tootsie & Roy.

The barn Oscar built for Grandpa Nels.

Roy, Beauty, Adolf, Hilda, Irene and Tootsie.

Hilda and Queenie bringing in the cows with barn in the background.

Olaf (Hilda's brother) & Emma (Olaf's wife).

Olaf & Hilda's cousins in Sweden.

Oscar's brother in Sweden-
Lar's Adolf Rosenberg & wife, Una.

Olaf & Hilda's cousins in Sweden

Neighbor's Sod House.

Cutting wheat. Alfred Swanson, Wilfred, and neighbor bachelor Nels holding a scythe.

Early farm machinery for harvesting ~ about 1915.

Irene & Roy

Irene, Roy & Adolf

Irene, Roy & Adolf
The vast Saskatchewan Prairie where the sky and the earth meet.

Evelyn and Wilford Swanson standing by their prairie house.

Roy, three of their farm horses and Irene on 'Lady.' The middle horse is eating from a feed bag.

Irene's prize entry - LITTLE RED HEN in freehand paper cutting contest.

Oscar's carpentry shop. Written on the back: "When we left Canada, Father sold it to him."

'Goodbye Prairie'
- The Little Prairie House, Roy, Irene, Queenie, Hilda & Adolf.

Shaunavon, Saskatchewan, Canada
1919

Grandpa Nels.

SS Princess Victoria, the beautiful, luxurious steamship.

Seattle - 1920
Irene, Hilda, Adolf, Roy and Oscar holding baby Violet.

Menagerie, Woodland Park postcard.

"Big Hair Bows"

Big Hair Bows were fashionable even before the Roaring Twenties.

Friends and neighborhood kids.
Their house is in the background.

Seattle - Early 1920's.

Violet, Adolf & Irene in a goat cart. Seattle *(via a traveling photographer)*.

Violet & Doll Buggy.

Irene with little Violet, unknown kids, and a 'Whole lotta chickens.'

Oscar with scythe in early 1920's.

Janet Moen

"Pals" early 1920's
Billy Siepmann and Adolf "Ade" Rosenberg.

Irene and her future husband, Bill.

Irene & Verna

"Bill with our Tommy horse and hay rake holding Harry and Janet."
1942

Janet, Harry and cousin Jerry making a windmill.

Irene and Bill.

Janet
High School
1956

Harry (3 years old),
Janet (9 months old)
1939.

Irene's Artwork from the 1940's

"Dancing Lady" sculpted from the clay found while digging our farm's well.

Pine Cones

Folk Art Horses.

My mother sold ceramics at the very first Bellevue Arts and Crafts Fair in 1947.

Camp Grande - Camano Island

"Tommy" painted in oil, and my father made the frame. Tommy was my father's workhorse and they worked all over the Eastside. He lived to be 33 years old and was a wonderful friend to grow up with.

Watercolors -

Bridle Trails

Tommy

The Lone Wolf

"When I was a little girl."

Written on the bottom of the picture:

Janet and pussy willows - Third Birthday -1942

Snowy Day

THE END

The Ultimate Workbook
for Preserving Your Legacy & You

Write Heart Memories®
Beth Lord

Available on www.bethlord.com & www.amazon.com
Online Support Step by Step

The Easy Way To Get Your Stories In A Book.

Write Heart Memories®

Beth Lord

Story Guide, Author, Therapist, and Founder

Write Heart Memories®Publishing Company

Personal Memoir making by DIY, Coaching, or Signature.
Fun & Easy.

206.929.0024 | www.bethlord.com

Made in the USA
Las Vegas, NV
21 September 2023

77887167R00070